NATIONAL GEOGRAPHIC

School Publishing

Destination: Moon

PATHFINDER EDITION

By Beth Geiger

CONTENTS

Flames burn under the rocket as you blast off. The engines roar. You're on your way to the moon. A few days later you are close to the moon's surface. The next step is to land. You pick a good spot and the lunar lander moves toward the surface. As you touch down your heart races. You're on the moon!

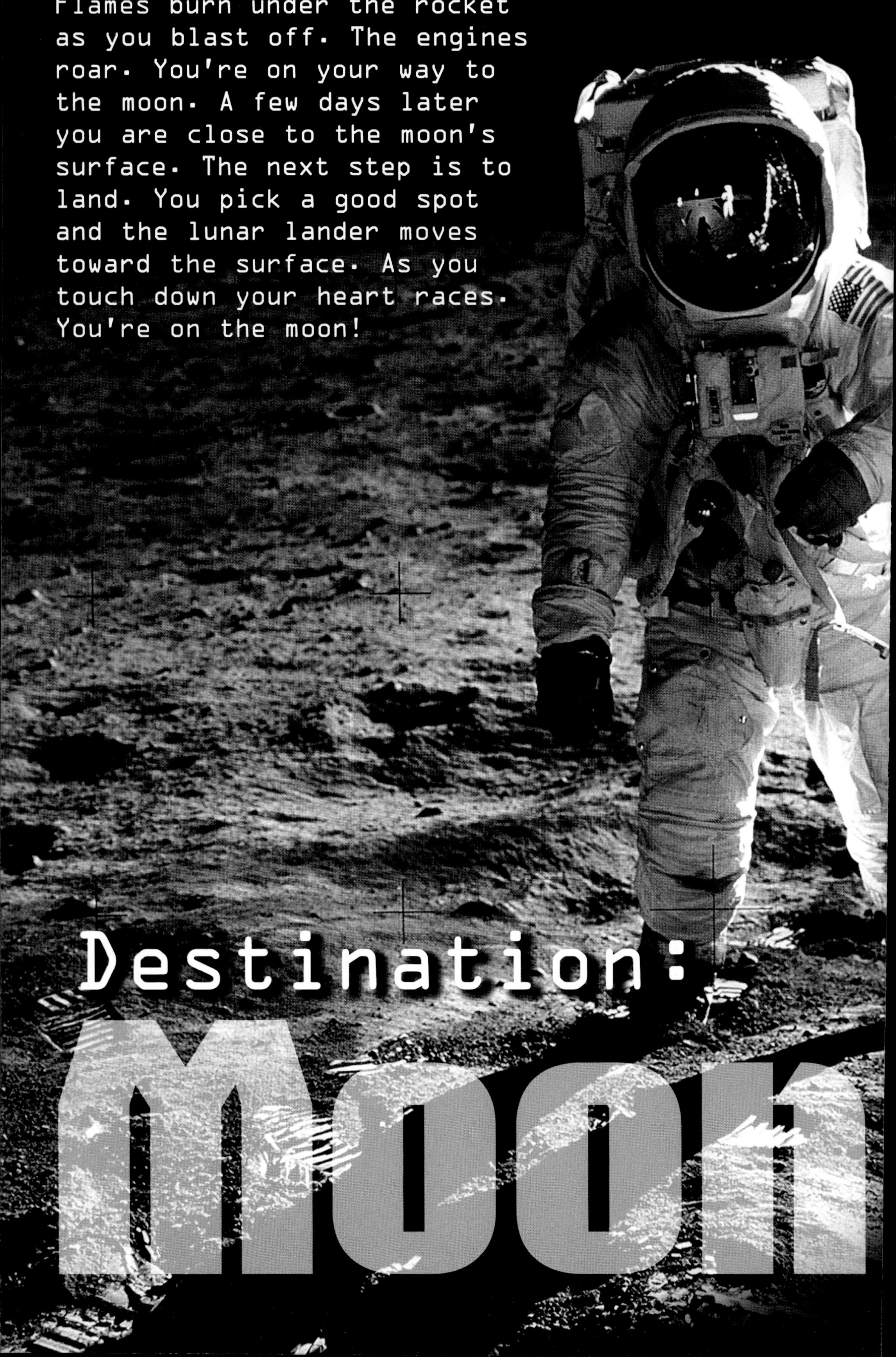

Destination: Moon

A Bold Plan

This may sound like a video game. But it happened. Between 1969 and 1972, NASA, the United States' Space Agency, successfully sent 12 people to the moon. Now NASA wants to go back to the moon. It is working on a plan called the Constellation Program. If the plan is approved it will have three parts.

The first part of the plan is to land on the moon by 2020. Scientists think that studying the moon will help us understand our planet better. Astronauts may also find minerals or gases there that could help with other space explorations.

The second part of the plan is to build a space base on the moon. Astronauts can stay there for months. That will give them more time to explore.

The third part is the boldest part: to use the moon base to go to the planet Mars.

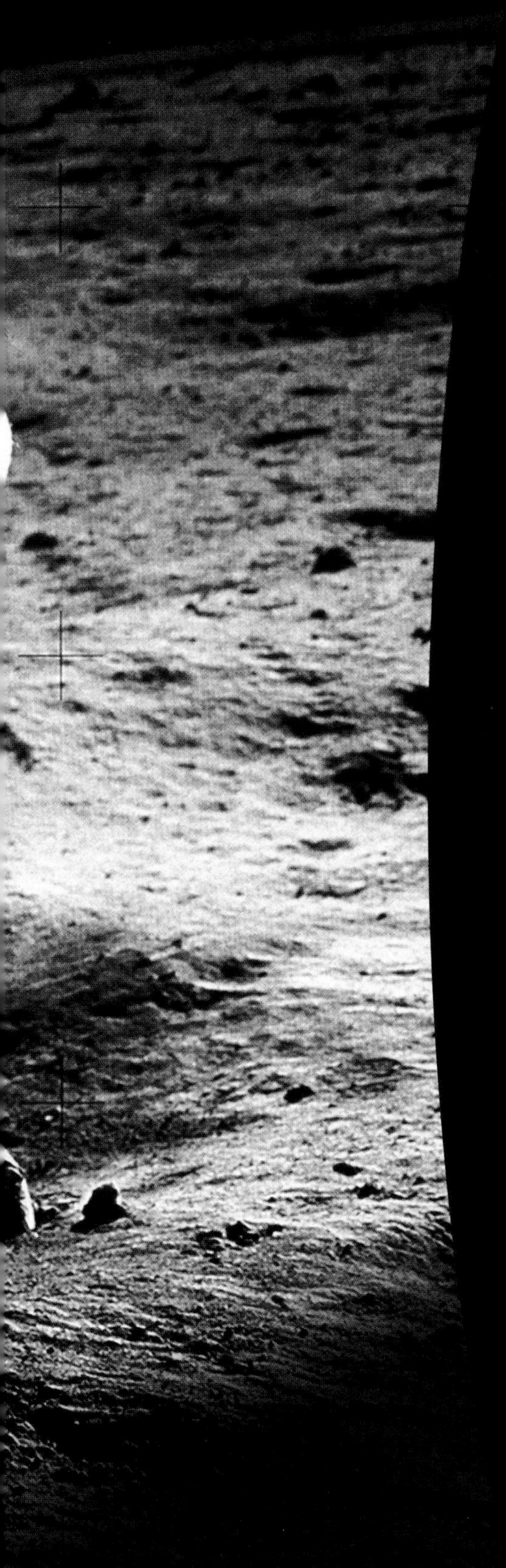

Moon Stats

Average Distance from Earth: 384,400 kilometers (238,555 miles). That's like circling Earth 10 times!

Size: 49 moons could fit inside Earth

Number of Days to Orbit Earth: 27.32

Speed of moon traveling around Earth: 3,682 kilometers (2,288 miles) per hour. That's 4 times faster than a jet passenger plane flies.

Highest surface temperature: 123° C (253° F). That's hot enough to cook meat.

First spacecraft to land on the moon: *Luna*, September 12, 1959

First human visit: *Apollo 11* (NASA) July 20, 1969

By Beth Geiger

A Big Push. The Ares V rocket will blast the lunar lander into space. It is 116 meters (381 feet) tall.

Part 1

Blastoff!

Scientists at NASA are already working on the first part of the plan. It will use two spacecraft for the trip to the moon. They will be called *Orion* and *Altair*.

First, a rocket will blast *Orion* into space from NASA's Kennedy Space Center in Florida. Four astronauts will travel inside. It will **orbit,** or circle around Earth, waiting for *Altair* to arrive.

Next, a rocket will blast *Altair* into space, too. *Altair* will carry the equipment. *Altair* will connect with *Orion*. Then both ships will travel to the moon together. When they get near, they will orbit the moon. Then, the astronauts move from *Orion* into *Altair*. *Altair* will be the spacecraft that lands on the moon. It is called a lunar lander.

The two spacecraft will separate, and *Altair* will take the equipment and the astronauts down to the moon. *Orion* will stay up in space orbiting the moon. The astronauts will explore the moon for a week. Then *Altair* will carry them back to *Orion*. *Orion* will take them back to Earth.

The flight back can be dangerous. When *Orion* enters Earth's atmosphere, **friction** between the spacecraft and the air will produce a lot of heat. *Orion* will have special heat shields to protect it.

Footprints on the moon stay forever! Why? There is no atmosphere, so there is no wind to blow them away.

Home Away From Home

In Part 2 of the Constellation Program, astronauts will build a space base on the moon.

NASA has some ideas about how to do this. Rockets without astronauts could carry large pieces of the base to the moon. These pieces are called **modules**. The modules will be made from light, strong material.

Altair will take astronauts and equipment to the moon. The design of the *Altair* spacecraft will include things scientists learned from the last moon missions. But, in other ways, it will be new. *Altair* will be bigger and will be made of lighter material.

Landing on the moon isn't exactly like parking a car! The moon's surface has thousands of deep craters. It is also rocky and uneven. To help the astronauts land safely, *Altair* will have super-accurate cameras on board. The pictures taken by the camera will help the astronauts steer to a safe, smooth landing spot.

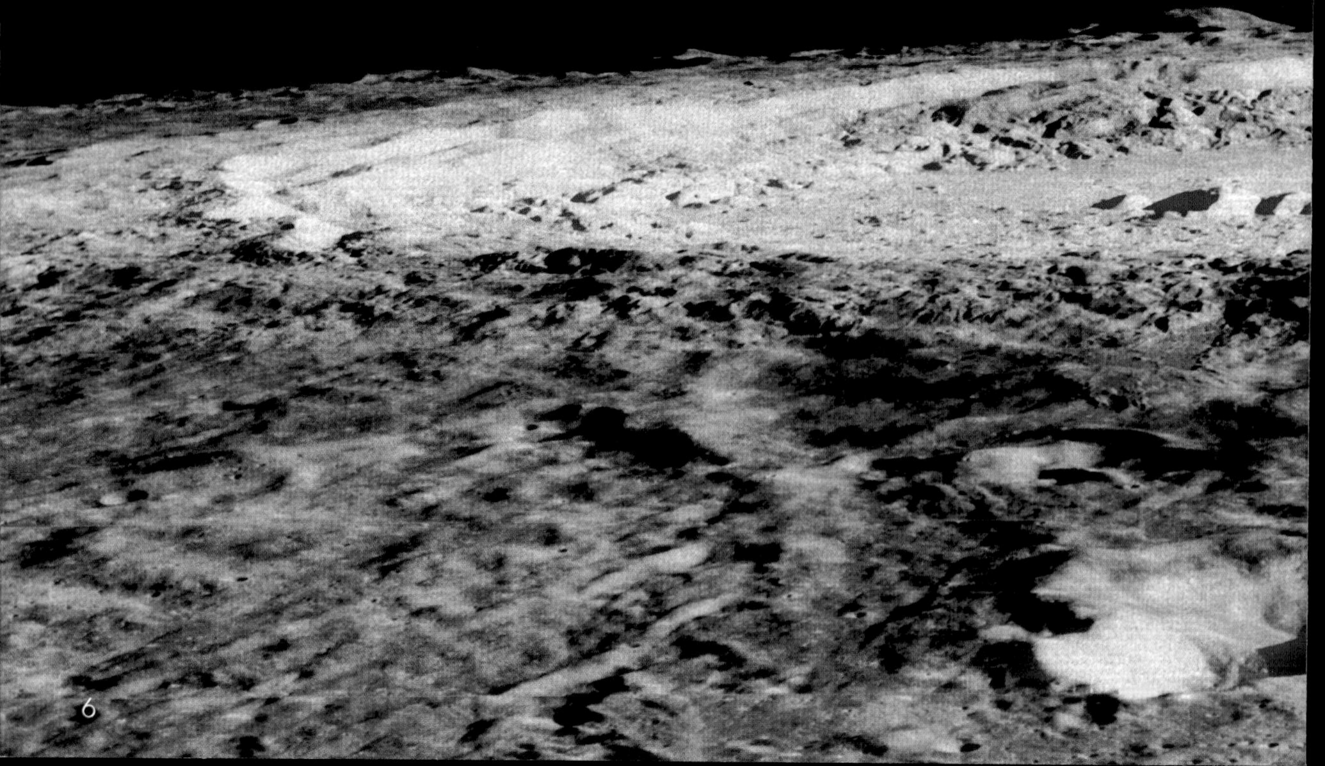

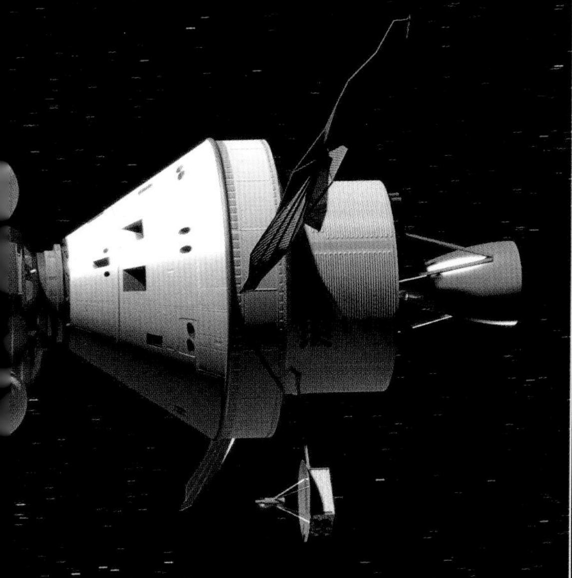

In Flight. This drawing shows *Orion* docked with *Altair* in space.

Searching for the Perfect Place

NASA will call the space base the Lunar Outpost. It is still looking for the perfect place to build it. The place must be smooth enough to build upon. It should be interesting to explore, too.

The South Pole of the moon might be just right. It is warmer than other parts of the moon. It gets a lot of sunlight, too. In 2009, scientists discovered that it even has water.

First, astronauts will stay at the space base for a week. Later, they will stay for six months.

Does the moon have days and nights?

Yes, very long days and nights! Each day lasts about 28.5 Earth days. At the lunar equator, that means 14 days of daylight, then 14 days of dark.

Life on the Moon

NASA has ideas for making life on the moon as comfortable as possible for astronauts. They will bring air and water from the Earth, but they might also find a way to use some from the moon. People don't weigh as much on the moon. So the astronauts will work out on special gym equipment. That way, their muscles and bones will stay healthy.

Space suits will be made extra tough. They have to hold up for a long time while astronauts explore the moon's rocky, dusty surface.

The moon gets a lot of sunshine. So solar panels will make energy. To get around, astronauts will drive a car called a Lunar Rover. It will be airtight. The astronauts could take off their space suits while inside. That will make working much easier.

The Moon's Matching Orbit and Rotation

The moon takes about 27 days to orbit Earth. It also takes about 27 days to revolve once.

Is this just chance? No! It's gravity. Earth's gravity pulls at the moon. This makes the moon bulge slightly in our direction. That bulge tends to stay where it is: facing Earth.

To see why this makes the moon's orbit and rotation the same, walk in a circle around a friend. Do exactly one "orbit," always facing your friend (you'll have to walk sideways). At the end of one orbit, notice that you have faced all directions. Not only have you orbited once, you've also rotated once.

Future Space Base. This drawing shows what the Lunar Outpost will probably look like.

Part 3

From the Moon to Mars!

The third part of the Constellation Program is really important. At this time NASA is planning to send rockets and astronauts to Mars. Gravity on the moon is much weaker than it is on Earth. This means rockets can lift off more easily from the moon. Still, a mission to Mars won't be simple or quick. It will take astronauts six months to travel there. Then they will stay on Mars for 18 months. Heading home will take another six months.

NASA's bold plan will not happen right away. There are some problems to be solved. But the people at NASA will work hard to do that so they can explore these areas.

Exploring Mars. This drawing shows a lunar lander on Mars.

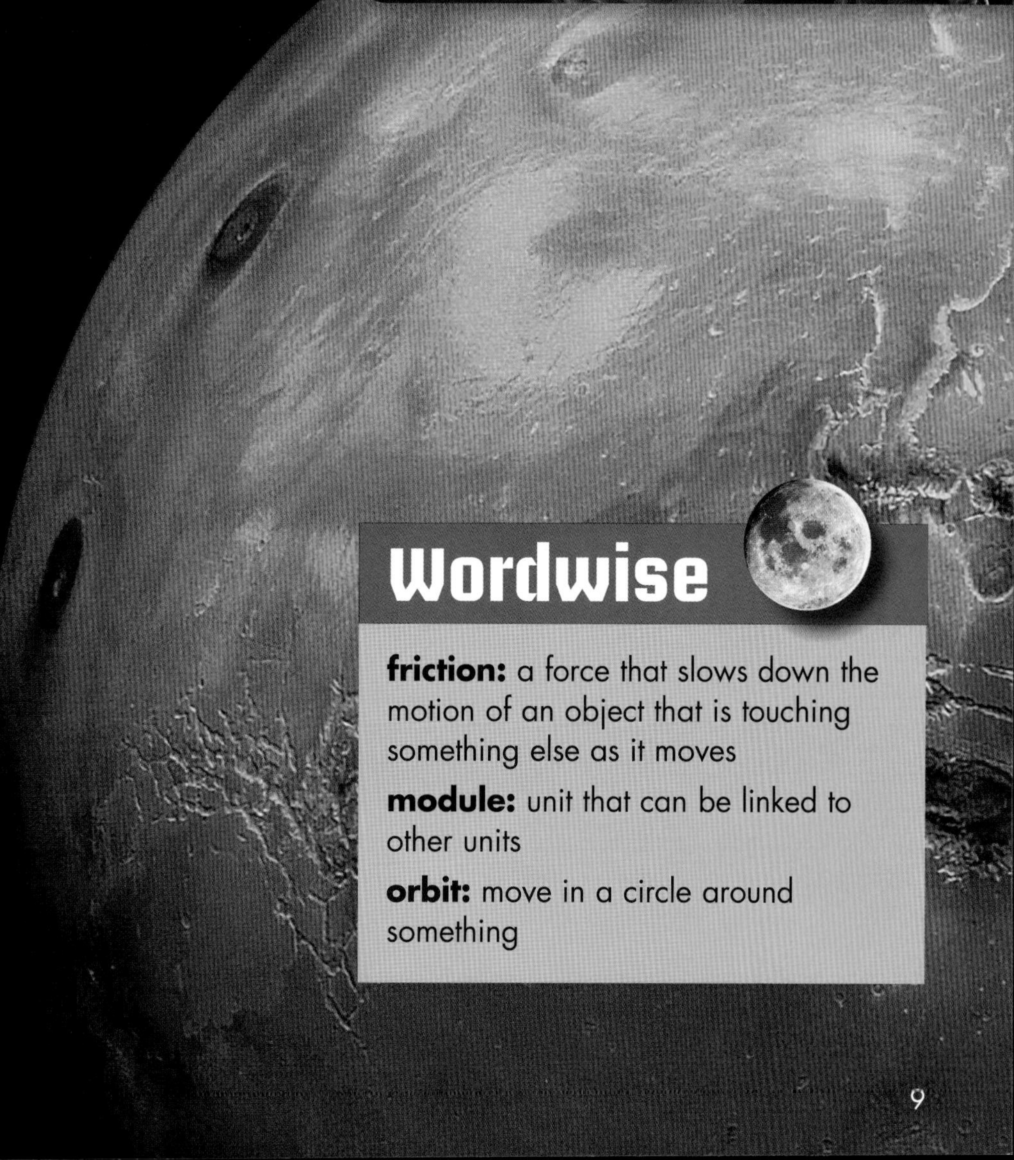

Wordwise

friction: a force that slows down the motion of an object that is touching something else as it moves

module: unit that can be linked to other units

orbit: move in a circle around something

The Right Stuff

No air. Extreme temperatures. Dangerous dust. Life on the moon won't exactly be easy. The NASA team is creating all the right stuff for this ultimate campout.

Practicing on Earth. That's just what NASA's special team of testers does. First, they head for Earth's most moon like spots...like deserts. Then they take the LER for a spin. They try out the latest space suits. They pretend to rescue each other. What a cool job!

Lunar Electric Rover (LER). These tough little 12-wheelers are made for overnight trips all over the moon. Wheels that turn allow the LER to drive on the moon's roughest terrain. Each LER will be about the size of a pickup truck. The inside of the LER is pressurized for safety and comfort. And the seats even unfold into beds!

Lunar habitats will be home sweet home for moon explorers. These are where the astronauts will live on the moon. The habitats must be light and modular, so they can be assembled on the moon. They must protect people from the strong sunlight and extreme temperatures. They have to have places to eat, sleep, and exercise. One idea is to make the habitats out of inflatable material. Solar power will provide energy.

Moon Adventures

Put yourself to the test by answering these questions about space exploration.

1. What are the three main parts of NASA's Constellation Program?
2. What conditions make living on the moon so difficult?
3. How are Earth and the moon different?
4. Why is NASA planning to launch rockets from the moon to Mars?
5. If you could invent something that would make life on the moon better, what would it be?